THE 10-PARAGRAPH
PRESS RELEASE©

DEBORAH A. L. FRIEND

Acknowledgements

I'd like to dedicate this book to everyone who has helped me get to where I am today – my family, friends and colleagues. With specific reference to the writing of this book, I would like to thank the following people: Corrie Gardner, for being the first person to tell me it was good; Wendy Eriksson, who helped me turn a manuscript into a real book; Anita Perryman for being a great proofreader; Sharon Smallwood and Mike Maloney for checking my journalism facts; and my wonderful, supportive husband, who is there beside me every step of the way.

©Write Away Whitsundays 2015. All rights reserved.
Text ©Deborah A. L. Friend
Photographs ©Deborah A. L. Friend
Illustrations ©Deborah A. L. Friend

Deborah A. L. Friend asserts the moral right to be identified as the author of this work.

Cover image Shutterstock

Printed edition first published in Australia 2015 by
Write Away Whitsundays
PO Box 340
Cannonvale
Queensland 4802
Australia

M: 0488 760 800
International: +61 488 760 800
E: deborah@writeawaywhitsundays.com.au
www.writeawaywhitsundays.com.au

National Library of Australia Cataloguing-in-Publication entry:

Friend, Deborah A. L., author.

The 10-paragraph press release : how to write press releases that will be published / Deborah A. L. Friend.

ISBN: 9780994215109 (paperback)

Press releases. Public relations.

659.2

Disclaimer: The material in this publication is of the nature of general comment only and does not represent professional advice. It is not intended to provide specific guidance for particular circumstances and should not be relied on as the basis for any decision to take action or not take action on any matters that it covers. Readers should obtain professional advice where appropriate before making any such decision. To the maximum extent permitted by law, the author and publisher disclaim all responsibility and liability to any person, arising directly or indirectly from any person taking or not taking action based on the information in this publication.

ISBN 978-0-9942151-0-9

Contents

Introduction   1

Who am I?   3

Why a Media Release?   5

Style   7

Paragraph One   10

The Five Ws and H   12

What?   13

When?   14

Who?   15

Where?   15

Why?   16

How?   17

First Paragraph in Summary   18

Paragraph Two   19

Paragraph Three   22

Paragraph Four   26

Paragraph Five   29

Paragraph Six   34

Paragraph Seven   37

Paragraphs Eight and Nine   40

Paragraph Ten   43

The 10-Paragraph Press Release© Complete   45

Conclusion   49

The 10-Paragraph Press Release© Check List   50

Sending Your Release   52

Pictures Paint a Thousand Words   54

Online Media Releases   55

And lastly…   58

Media Release: Calling all Bread Bakers,
Cheese Makers and Food Creators   60

Media Release: Whitsunday Marine Academy
Featured on TV's Getaway-from-it-all   62

Media Release: Birthday Bonanza Continues
Unabated – More Than a Third off Selected
Sailing Holidays   64

Bonus Section   67

News Values   68

Tight Writing   71

Additional Information for Journalists   72

Introduction

Press releases – also called news releases and media releases – are one way in which anyone, from large corporations to individuals, can transmit their news to the media and thus the public.

Whether you are a communications professional, a small business owner, a charity or a not-for-profit, a well written media release can help you get your message out there and sell your idea, cause, product or organisation.

Of course, the idea is that the media you have targeted will publish or broadcast your release in some fashion.

By writing your release in a way that journalists favour, you can enhance your chances of it, firstly, being read by the journalist or editor and, secondly, being published (or broadcast).

Why is this? It is for several reasons, mostly to do with a reporter's lack of time and resources.

A well written media release means less re-working is required, which saves the journalist time. A well written release will also grab his or her attention, especially if it has a catchy headline.

In busy newsrooms, half the battle is catching the gatekeeper's attention.

A well written release is also more likely to be passed on to fellow reporters who cover that particular area (who in their right mind would forward their colleagues badly written copy?).

In short, they are far less likely to hit the bin.

In this book, I will show you, paragraph by paragraph, how to write a media release that will give you the best chance of being published.

Your release might not be reproduced word-for-word – and indeed, it would be a worry if all press releases were – but it will be 'picked up' by journalists, who will then, possibly, add their own slant.

A well written media release can also find its way into feature stories (along with other organisations, products etc.) or can provide 'expert comment' for an ongoing news topic.

Or it might just spark a media debate. Whatever the outcome of your media release, it needs to represent you and your organisation in the best possible light.

And this book is going to show you how to do that in a simple 10-step format.

Why 10 paragraphs? Most media releases should be about 300 words (maximum 400 if it is a complex topic). A paragraph should be no more than 30 words, so 10 paragraphs gives you 300 words.

Check out newspapers and the length of their stories – you will be surprised how few words a lot of them contain and therein lies the skill of the journalist.

I hope this book helps aspiring communications professionals, as well as business owners, not-for-profits, volunteers working for charities and just about anyone who needs a helping hand getting their message out there.

Who am I?

Who am I and why do I think I can help you write better media releases?

I started my career with a degree in marketing and after some time working in marketing and advertising, I moved 'left field' into journalism, which I loved.

I was lucky enough to work as a reporter on a busy, daily newspaper in the UK for four years, where I also studied for the UK journalism qualification.

This is where I honed my writing skills and most of what I am going to share with you was learnt during these years tied to a computer for nine hours a day, six days a week.

Whilst there, I wrote more than one million words of copy (based on 1,000 words a day, which was normal practice) and saw literally thousands of media releases – some good, some atrocious, many of them very average.

From journalism, I bounced into public relations, where I am now on the 'other side of the fence' when it comes to writing media releases for my clients (which I hope will be taken up by journalists).

I still use my journalism skills all the time and I like to think it is these skills that help get my clients' media releases published. Or at least sufficiently interest a journalist to get him or her to take up the story.

Because of my background in print journalism, the way I write releases is very much geared to that medium but I have found that a well written release (along the lines I am going to explain to you) is also welcomed by radio and TV, who are more likely to use it as a basis for a story involving several sources.

Media releases for online news providers, lifestyle and travel websites and so on should also be written much the same way, with special attention given to keywords – especially in the headline and first paragraph – and hyperlinks.

I hope you enjoy reading this book and if you have any questions about anything contained in these pages, please do not hesitate to email me at questions@writeawaywhitsundays.com.au or check out Facebook.com/writeawaywhitsundays.

Happy writing.

Deborah A. L. Friend.

Deborah is owner/director of Write Away Whitsundays, a communications consultancy in the Whitsundays, North Queensland, Australia. www.writeawaywhitsundays.com.au

NOTE: All news story examples used in this book were taken – with permission – from the Sunday Mail, dated December 30, 2012.

Why a Media Release?

Before we get into the guts of writing your release, let's take a moment to actually think about what a media or press release is.

Also called a news release, I think the first point to note is that they must contain news.

This might sound like stating the obvious, but believe me, many so-called news releases do not contain news at all.

Quite often, they are a blatant advertisement for a product or service. These kinds of releases might, at best, end up in a feature but you can bet you will get a call from the advertising rep before the journalist calls you. At worst, they will end up in the bin.

News is a difficult thing to tie down and a complete analysis is beyond the scope of this book but a list of 'news values' has been included at the end of the book to assist you (see Bonus Section).

I think the important thing is that news can mean different things to different industry sectors. A new product for a tourism operator is certainly news in the tourism industry and a cutting-edge new packing line is certainly news in engineering and manufacturing trade publications.

Business wins, changing premises, new senior management, innovative partnerships, takeovers and industry visits are all news in the corporate world.

Writing a good media release is about knowing your audience – who are you trying to talk to and which media will best help you achieve this?

You need to think about your audience when writing your release, in order to achieve the right tone and style. The style and tone for a media release about skateboarding, for example, would be different to the way you would write a piece about superannuation for a finance magazine.

However, there are 'universal' style points that apply to all media releases and I am going to run you through a summary of media release style points and then we will jump into the 10-Paragraph Press Release©.

Style

Style is a funny thing and, as mentioned, you would adapt your style according to your specific audience and the medium that you are targeting your audience through.

There are, however, certain universal guidelines when it comes to media release writing style. Most of them (if not all) are long-established protocols, created in the first instance by the print media and, since then, adapted to suit other media.

These 'universal truths' are as follows:

- Use short sentences wherever possible. Do not tie the reader up in long, rambling sentences. Say it clearly and succinctly (this is known as 'tight' writing).

- Try and stick to one sentence per paragraph (there are exceptions to this rule if you are explaining a complex concept or difficult issue but, by and large, it should be one sentence or 'thought' per paragraph).

- Less is more. Do not use long, complicated words or phrases where a shorter word or less complicated phrase will do equally well. Hence, you do not say 'he was able to…' you say 'he could…'. You do not say 'they were in attendance' you say 'they were there'. See Bonus Section for more examples of achieving brevity.

- Use the active not passive voice. This gives your release strength, punch, authority. It is not always possible to achieve this but you should strive for it. A noticeable exception to the rule is when journalists use phrases such as 'it was revealed that…' or 'a report has been published…'.

- Always use the third person (he, she, they) never you, we, us etc. which are better left for social media and websites. Writing in the third person gives your release both authority and a certain distance (the latter being vital for objectivity).

- Try and use strong, punchy verbs. There is no need to go over the top but when the occasion calls for it, verbs such as slammed or ripped into (instead of criticises), drives up or boosts (instead of raises), deals a blow, urges, cripples, bans…you get the idea. But be sparing otherwise you will end up sounding like the worst 'trashy' magazine!

- Be precise. This is not an excuse to be too verbose (see 'less is more' above) but remember, you are painting a picture. So, rather than saying 'the bridge was several hundred metres high' find out exactly how high it is. Two hundred metres high is very different to five hundred metres. This will save the journalist having to do unnecessary work (giving your release a greater chance of publication) and also paints a picture for your reader. Similarly, a crowd of 50 is vastly different to 500 or 5,000 or 50,000 people. Which is it?

- People love figures. So give precise ages, miles travelled, monetary value, length of tunnel, height of the mast, number of visitors… Don't be vague and wishy-washy – give the reader facts.

- Correct spelling, punctuation and grammar. I have put this under 'style' because poor spelling, punctuation and grammar really are very poor style indeed. In the days of instant online dictionaries, there really is no excuse for bad spelling. Or keep an 'old-fashioned' dictionary by your computer – I do. If you are not 100 per cent comfortable with your mastery of punctuation and/or grammar, do a course, a webinar or read one of the many books available on the subject. Your writing style will certainly thank you for it (and you will increase the chances of getting your release published).

- Misspelling people's names. This is a writing sin – especially if they are your own people. And the misspelling of place names is a close second. You cannot expect the journalist to know the correct spelling of towns and streets – it is up to you to check.

- Don't over punctuate. Punctuation should help the reader better understand, not obstruct or slow them down. But there are certainly cases where you must punctuate, especially when it comes to commas (I would say, in general, they are left out too much rather than over used).

- And finally, if you want to adhere to journalistic convention, dates are Sunday, June 28, 2015 (not Sunday 28th June) and numbers are written out in full from one to nine and then numerically ie. 10, 11, 12 etc. If a number starts a sentence, spell it out in full eg. One hundred people attended the concert (not 100).

So that's a word about style. There are many more style points but the above should provide a handy check list to get you started.

Ready to start writing the actual content of your media release?

OK, let's go…

Paragraph One

It should come as no surprise that your opening paragraph – or 'intro' – is the single most important paragraph of the release.

Assuming you are trying to write like a journalist, your opening paragraph is what grabs the reader's attention (and tells readers whether they want to read more or not).

Moreover, because the journalist is looking for stories his readers will like, you will also grab his attention. Journalists and editors spend no more than a few minutes checking out a release to see if it is of interest – that first paragraph is all important.

It should be short, sharp and to the point (30 words maximum and preferably 25) while also summing up the story. It is no wonder journalists can spend as much time writing their intro as they do on the rest of the story.

In newspaper writing, the first paragraph should summarise the story for the reader.

Hence:

Japan's new Prime Minister Shinzo Abe has sought to expand the Japan-US security partnership to Australia and India as it faces a bitter territorial row with China.

[Editor's Note: I personally would have added a comma after India, but there you go.]

Notice how the intro still manages to be short and punchy (28 words) while summing up the crux of the story.

The rest of the story backs up this statement and expands on it (mainly through quoting Mr Abe).

Try to be as interesting as possible in your intro, while obviously sticking to the facts (it sounds like stating the obvious but start with the most interesting points of your story).

Hence:

The top pay-out by the nation's largest private health fund this year was almost $650,000 – for prostate surgery on a 70-year-old.

The story then goes on to talk about the 10 most expensive patient claims for 2012 – citing other examples – but the journalist has singled out the largest dollar amount for his intro.

You can also have fun with your intro (depending on the subject matter of course), as this journalist did with the following story about environmental complaints to council skyrocketing in the past year, including noisy animals (which accounted for almost half of all complaints).

Owners of noisy pets are in the doghouse after Queenslanders spent the year yapping at council about their pet peeves.

Very clever. Although you would obviously only use this kind of style for less 'serious' topics.

The Five Ws and H

It is pertinent at this point to mention the five Ws and H of journalism.

Quite simply, this is the Who, What, Where, Why, When and How of storytelling. These are the questions the reader asks himself.

Convention therefore dictates that the journalist should answer these questions for the reader. And the most pertinent questions should be answered in the first, second or third paragraph.

This is in case the story gets cut (which they often do). The main thrust of the story will still remain in the first three paragraphs.

The five Ws and one H are not just something journalists have made up. These questions are the questions people ask themselves when they hear about something.

So, for example, you are in the pub, waiting for your mate and she rushes in exclaiming 'sorry I'm late but there was an accident…'.

The first thing you ask is: Where was the accident, how did it happen, when was this? You might ponder why it happened and ask yourself if you could possibly know who was involved (the what in this instance is, of course, the accident itself).

It's natural to want to know the answers to these questions. So journalists give readers the answers to these questions as they build their story. Once you understand this, you can use the Ws and H as a check list to make sure you have represented the story in the first three paragraphs.

Whether you put the Who, the What, the How, the When, the Why or the Where in the first paragraph (and which of these fall into paragraphs two and three or even further down the story) is a matter of skill and judgement and I give you some pointers about this below.

Quite often, it is the What, the Who, the When and the Where in the opening paragraph (if not all four, then at least two or three of the four). Whichever of these does not come in the first paragraph will be included in the second or third paragraph. The Why and How might come in the first three paragraphs but quite often they come later as they are more complex questions to answer (often requiring more words).

What?

The What can be an accident, a heart transplant, an event, the publication of a report, an outbreak, an investigation or even the weather, as in this intro…

Perfect beach weather and school holidays were a winning combination for three Brisbane boys on the Gold Coast yesterday.

This is obviously a 'soft' news story and goes on to talk about the hot weather expected over the next few days. Mentioning the boys gives it more 'human interest'.

The What in any story is very important – it's the crux of the story – and it is a good idea to ask yourself before you start writing your opening paragraph: What is going on here? Why am I writing this release? What is my story? What is the angle I am going to take?

The answer to those questions should give you your opening paragraph.

So for example…

Parents can expect a back-to-school January cash splash from the Gillard Government with payments of up to $820 for every child.

No doubt this story would have come from a long-winded government media release with plenty of figures included. The journalist has scanned down the release and found what she hopes is of most interest to her readers – the $820 'cash splash'.

Notice also how she starts with 'parents can expect…' instantly drawing readers in (a less experienced journalist might have started with 'Federal Government family payments were announced recently'…boring).

When?

In the example above, the When is January and is integral to the story. Parents obviously want to know when they will receive this 'cash splash' – so it is included in the first paragraph.

When can be very important – as in the case of most accidents and deaths (you would think it a bit strange if you first heard about a fatal accident or the death of a well known politician a week after it happened).

Or When can be unimportant – if something happened a while ago and the journalist is now doing a follow-up, the original 'when' might come further down the story (along with more background etc.).

Note: With follow-ups (further developments on an ongoing story or issue), the journalist will focus firstly on the 'here and now' – the most recent happenings (news is "now") – and will then trickle out to previous happenings or events.

If the When happened a while ago, 'bury' it further down your media release (unless of course it is still relevant, as in 'An investigation that closed more than 30 years ago is now being reopened due to…').

Who?

It is important to remember that Who is not just a person. In a news writing sense, it can also be an organisation, a charity, a government, a council or even a product.

This does not mean that you call the organisation 'who' – it is still 'which' – it just means that the Who of your story is not necessarily a person, as in the following example.

Retail giant Low-Price is set to spark a petrol price war as it forges ahead with a plan to roll out its own discount fuel outlets.

In this intro, the Who is Low-Price. The What is a petrol price war. Note: This is a good example of the journalist sitting back and asking herself 'what is going on here?'.

She could have settled for the What being Low-Price's plan to roll out its own discount fuel outlets. But with the help of a great quote from fuel price monitor FUELtrac – the spokesperson was quoted as saying the plan would 'ramp up the already fierce supermarket price wars' – the What becomes the petrol price war in this story.

The Who can also be plural and sometimes a little 'vague'…

Three-quarters of bachelor degree graduates find full-time work within four months of completing their studies, new figures show.

The journalist, of course, goes on to clarify who these graduates are but a more generalised Who can sometimes be used to good effect in intros.

Where?

Where is important because it anchors the story for a reader. It sounds harsh, but we are more likely to be concerned about an earthquake in our own country than we would about one on the other side of the world, unless we have friends or family travelling there (the Where is quite strongly associated with the news value of 'impact' – does this impact on me or someone I know?).

Stories about natural disasters, bush fires, floods etc. only start to mean something when we know where they are happening.

Accidents and deaths usually require a Where fairly early on in the story – you would think it strange if a journalist told you a body had been discovered but not where – and of course events and physical happenings, such as the local Member of Parliament making a speech, require a Where.

Stories about investigations being launched or reports being published do not require a Where in the opening paragraph because it is not as pertinent (it might come later in the story or maybe not at all).

Why?

Why is a little more tricky and quite often it will be left until further down the story to explain the Why to the reader (the answer to Why is often more complex than the other four Ws).

However, this is not always the case…

A police officer was taken to hospital with non-life threatening injuries after a stolen car rammed his motorbike near the Gold Coast.

The police officer (who) was taken to hospital (what) because his motorbike was rammed by a stolen car (why). In this instance, the Why is very relevant to the story and so it goes in the first paragraph.

How?

Perhaps even more complex than Why, the How is often borne out later in the story when the journalist has the luxury of a few more words to 'put his case'.

If you cannot get your How into your first three paragraphs, do not worry. Instinct – and practice – should tell you when your How is necessary.

Sometimes it does form part of the crux of the story and will therefore appear in your first paragraph…

Nearly 300 motorists have been caught not wearing seat belts in Queensland in the past six days as police continue a blitz.

Nearly 300 motorists (who) have been caught not wearing seat belts (what) in Queensland (where) in the past six days (when) as police continue a blitz (how were they caught?).

Practice makes perfect

The above pointers about the five Ws and one H of journalism are just a summary of how and when each is used. I could fill an entire book and still not cover every configuration.

The only way you will become proficient is by practising.

Read stories in the newspapers you are targeting and try and identify which Ws come in the first paragraph and which in the second and third paragraphs (or later in the story). Ask yourself, why has the journalist written it like this? You will find it is all about relevance, pertinence and interest.

First paragraph in summary...

So to summarise your first paragraph (also known as the intro or lead)…

Short and to the point, while also summarising the story.

This will entail answering some (the most pertinent) of the five Ws and one H for the reader.

It should also be interesting enough to grab the reader's attention (and hence also the journalist's or editor's attention).

It should set the scene for the rest of the story (if you have summarised the story in the first paragraph this should happen naturally).

Note: In the world of newspapers, the headline is pulled, more often than not, from the opening paragraph, so if it doesn't summarise the story, neither will the headline.

Paragraph Two

So having now briefly explained the five Ws and one H and the importance of your first paragraph, we continue with our 10-Paragraph Press Release© and look at paragraph two.

Paragraph two expands on what you have already started to say in paragraph one, backing it up, providing more facts and clarification.

Remember, paragraph one is all about impact so you might have gone for a more generalised intro to get your point across. Or you might have plucked out the most interesting point to grab attention.

You now need to expand on what you said in paragraph one and you do that by adding facts and names.

Hence, in our earlier example about health fund payouts, the journalist goes with the latter tactic ie. plucking out the most interesting point to grab attention.

1   *The top pay-out by the nation's largest private health fund this year was almost $650,000 – for prostate surgery on a 70-year-old.*

The journalist follows this up with a second paragraph explaining where the figures came from and the reason for their publication...

2   *Medibank released its list of the top 10 most expensive claims for 2012, highlighting how the health costs of the elderly are driving up premiums and putting pressure on national finances.*

In paragraph two, the journalist answers the Who more specifically (ie. Medibank is mentioned – in the first paragraph this was a more generalised 'the nation's largest private health fund').

Also answered are the What (released its top 10 most expensive claims for 2012) and the Why (they wanted to highlight the fact the health costs of the elderly are pushing up premiums).

This begs the question, which of the five Ws were in the first paragraph and, in truth, it is a difficult one to answer because this is more of a 'dropped' intro – an attention-grabber with more information unfolding in paragraph two.

There is also a kind of When in paragraph two, as we are informed the claims were during 2012, which anchors it for us (it would be a different story altogether if the figures were 10 years old).

Another example of paragraph two expanding on paragraph one follows:

1 *Queensland taxpayers will be stung by a phone bill of at least $60 million for calls bureaucrats never make.*

2 *The Sunday Mail can reveal that a whole-of-government telecommunications deal signed in 2011 commits the current administration to a prescribed level of annual expenditure.*

Notice how in paragraph two, the journalist expands on paragraph one by explaining that the reason the taxpayers are going to be stung by a phone bill of at least $60m (ie. the Why) is because the government signed a deal committing them to a prescribed amount ['level of annual expenditure'].

We still don't know why the bureaucrats did not actually make the calls but we are getting there (the story is opening up). We also have our When answered in paragraph two.

Similarly...

1 *The State Government will allow rent deferrals for leasehold farmers and businesses in fire-ravaged north Queensland.*

2 *The decision could affect up to 80 landholders in the Etheridge and Tableland shires.*

The journalist has given the reader more detail in paragraph two to back up what he said in paragraph one (whilst also creating an interesting intro – notice the use of the word 'fire-ravaged').

In paragraph two, we now know how many landholders could be affected (remember, figures paint a picture) and precisely where these landholders are located.

So in two paragraphs, we have our What (rent deferrals for farmers), Who (State Government) and Where (Etheridge and Tableland shires).

I would suggest we also have our Why, as it is implied (and understood by the reader) that the deferrals are because the landholders have been affected by bush fires (and the government wants to give them a bit of a break).

You might ask yourself why, in this story, the Who is not the landholders. My answer would be that the Who is (most times) the do-er of the sentence ie. the subject (not the object, which is the person or thing having something done to them).

Paragraph Three

As already mentioned, you are trying to summarise your entire story in three paragraphs, so in paragraph three you must answer the remaining Ws and H (subject to the limitations mentioned above).

So, in our example about rent deferrals for landholders affected by bush fires, we are given more detail in paragraph three that starts to explain how this is going to work, as follows…

1   *The State Government will allow rent deferrals for leasehold farmers and businesses in fire-ravaged north Queensland.*

2   *The decision could affect up to 80 landholders in the Etheridge and Tableland shires.*

3   *The deferral will be for the 2012-13 financial year but will include an interest rate of two per cent.*

If this story was chopped at this point (it wasn't but we will discuss paragraphs four and five a bit later on) it would still stand on its own – the reader has enough facts in three paragraphs to know the basis of what is going on with regards to this story.

So in essence, your first three paragraphs should summarise your whole story, for example…

1   *Scientists have discovered nerve cells that deal solely with itching in a major breakthrough for pain relief. It could lead to new anti-itch treatments.*

2   *Many experts had previously thought that the receptors for pain and itching were linked.*

3   *However, the team from John Hopkins University found that certain nerve cells are specialised to detect itchy sensations – and those receptors don't detect pain.*

In the first three paragraphs of this story the journalist answers the Who (scientists), the What (discovery of nerve cells that deal solely with itching) and the Where (John Hopkins University).

The journalist has also included in the intro '…in a major break-through for pain relief', which adds impact (the reader thinks 'thank goodness, some relief from pain, at last…'). Notice the use of strong words such as 'major' and 'breakthrough' in the opening paragraph (attention-grabbing).

I would suggest the Why is also answered - Why is this discovery so important? Well, for years, experts thought receptors for pain and itching were linked.

The When is not mentioned (the journalist has made a decision that this is not as important as Who, What, Where and Why in this instance).

TOP TIP	Do not try and shoehorn all five Ws and the H into the first three paragraphs if it doesn't work. You are trying to entertain, inform and educate your reader – not bang them over the head with excruciating sentence construction so you can get all your Ws and H in.

The How in this story is obviously very complex (the discovery probably took years of tests and experiments) and there is no place for it in a three paragraph story (remember, many stories are cut to three paragraphs and must 'stand alone').

However, had the story run its entire length, I am sure the How would have been dealt with (even if only in summary form).

A good example of summing up in three paragraphs what could have been a boring story is our previous example about the bureaucrats' phone bills…

1   *Queensland taxpayers will be stung by a phone bill of at least $60 million for calls bureaucrats never make.*

2   *The Sunday Mail can reveal that a whole-of-government telecommunications deal signed in 2011 commits the current administration to a prescribed level of annual expenditure.*

3   *However, public servants are not texting, dialling or Googling anywhere near enough to meet the 'committed spend' contract, which does not expire until mid-2014.*

The What in this story is the fact that the taxpayers (Who) will be stung by a $60m phone bill.

Remember what we said previously about stepping back and asking yourself 'what is going on here?'.

A less experienced journalist could have made the telecommunications deal the What but this journalist has very cleverly asked himself, what does this mean to my readers? His conclusion is that Queensland taxpayers (notice how he instantly draws us in) will be stung (strong, powerful word) by a $60 million phone bill (figures get people's attention – especially large monetary ones).

He has plucked out the essence of the story for his first paragraph, as it pertains to his readers.

We then need the second paragraph to expand a little on the first paragraph – how is this so? – and clarify things for us.

Notice how the third paragraph then goes on to 'wrap it up' by expanding on why the bureaucrats are not making the calls and therefore not meeting the committed spend. It also adds more drama by advising the reader that the contract does not expire until mid-2014.

Note the interesting use of the When in this story – one in the past and one in the future – as the journalist felt (correctly, I feel) that it was of interest to the reader to know when the contract expires, as well as when it was first signed.

The other point to make about the third paragraph is that, quite often, it sets up the conflict of the story (conflict being one of the major news values, of course).

So, in the above example, the first two paragraphs set the scene and then the third paragraph explains why it is an issue. Notice how the third paragraph starts with the word 'however'.

A lot of third paragraphs start with the word 'however', as in…this has happened (paragraphs one and two), however (paragraph three) it is an issue or a problem because…

Paragraph Four

Paragraph four is important as it is when the reader decides if he/she is going to continue reading.

Obviously, as the writer of the media release you hope that they do, as this is when you are able to include some of your key messages, in support of your business, product, cause, event etc.

Paragraph four is the 'bridging' paragraph. You must create a bridge between your first three paragraphs (summarising the crux of your story) and the remainder of the story, where you will give more detail to support and substantiate the first three paragraphs.

The best way of doing this is to introduce your spokesperson, telling the reader who they are and what they do (normally their title) and also their 'relevance' to the story (why are they speaking?).

At the same time, you are starting to add detail.

So, for example, in the previous story about the major breakthrough discovery that certain nerve cells are specialised to detect itchy sensations...

1   *Scientists have discovered nerve cells that deal solely with itching in a major breakthrough for pain relief. It could lead to new anti-itch treatments.*

2   *Many experts had previously thought that the receptors for pain and itching were linked.*

3   *However, the team from John Hopkins University found that certain nerve cells are specialised to detect itchy sensations – and those receptors don't detect pain.*

4   *"Itch-specific neurones have been sought for decades," the researchers say in their paper, published in Nature Neuroscience.*

The quote adds a kind of When ('for decades') and is also the "payoff" to the intro, as it explains why this is a 'major breakthrough'.

Giving the source of the published data adds authority and credibility to the story and ties it down for the reader (they are not just vague findings, they are actually published in Nature Neuroscience).

[Notice also the use of 'however' again at the start of paragraph three.]

Picking up on another of our earlier examples that demonstrates this bridging technique…

1   *The State Government will allow rent deferrals for leasehold farmers and businesses in fire-ravaged north Queensland.*

2   *The decision could affect up to 80 landholders in the Etheridge and Tableland shires.*

3   *The deferral will be for the 2012-13 financial year but will include an interest rate of two per cent.*

4   *Minister for Natural Resources and Mines Andrew Cripps said graziers and small business owners in shires declared under natural disaster arrangements and whose property has sustained damage due to fire, could apply for deferral of leasehold land rent.*

In the fourth paragraph, we are introduced to our spokesperson and, because of his title, the reader understands why Mr Cripps is being quoted (his title explains his relevance).

In this indirect quote (see Top Tip below for the difference between direct and indirect quotes) we are given more detail, which backs up the statements made in the first two paragraphs.

Hence...

...graziers and small business owners (expanding on 'landholders') in shires declared under natural disaster arrangements (clarifying exactly who is eligible) and whose property has sustained damage due to fire (backing up the more general 'fire-ravaged' in the intro) could apply for deferral of leasehold land rent.

In our earlier story about the bureaucrats' phone bills, the journalist has used the fourth paragraph to start adding more detail and to provide 'evidence' to support the statements made in paragraphs one to three. The quotes come a bit later (it is quite a long story) and the journalist has chosen (rightly, I feel) to add some substantiating facts first.

1   *Queensland taxpayers will be stung by a phone bill of at least $60 million for calls bureaucrats never make.*

2   *The Sunday Mail can reveal that a whole-of-government telecommunications deal signed in 2011 commits the current administration to a prescribed level of annual expenditure.*

3   *However, public servants are not texting, dialling or Googling anywhere near enough to meet the 'committed spend' contract, which does not expire until mid-2014.*

4   *The Newman Government has confirmed it received a $15.3 million bill from Optus for under-spent telecommunication services in 2011.*

TOP TIP	A direct quote is one contained in quotation marks with he/she/they said after it (or before it, depending on the publication's style). An indirect quote has no quotation marks and will start with the name of the person, who said...
	Indirect quotes are useful for paraphrasing long-winded direct quotes and presenting them in a more concise readable format.

Paragraph Five

Given what we have talked about above, it will come as no surprise that paragraph five is your quote (as well as paragraph six and possibly also paragraph seven depending how much you have to say on a topic, but more on that a bit later).

So in our story about rent deferrals for fire-affected farmers, the fourth paragraph sets up the spokesperson and the fifth paragraph is the spokesperson's quote.

1   *The State Government will allow rent deferrals for leasehold farmers and businesses in fire-ravaged north Queensland.*

2   *The decision could affect up to 80 landholders in the Etheridge and Tableland shires.*

3   *The deferral will be for the 2012–13 financial year but will include an interest rate of two per cent.*

4   *Minister for Natural Resources and Mines Andrew Cripps said graziers and small business owners in shires declared under natural disaster arrangements and whose property has sustained damage due to fire, could apply for deferral of leasehold land rent.*

5   *"Fires have destroyed vast tracts of grazing land in the Etheridge Shire Council and Tablelands Regional Council areas," Mr Cripps said.*

Notice how the quote adds some emotion, with the words 'destroyed' and 'vast' being used.

When you are writing your media release, your quote is all important. This is for several reasons:

It is your chance to say exactly what you want to say and get your message across as you see it.

Of all the bits of your media release that a journalist can chop and edit, the quotation is really the most sacred, as journalistic convention dictates you should not interfere with the meaning of a quote. That is not to say quotes don't get chopped – of course they do – but the meaning must remain the same.

It is precisely because your quote is your chance to say exactly what you want on a subject, that it should not be abused and should be used wisely.

By abused, I mean do not use quotes for gratuitous 'sales' messages and/or statements that are irrelevant to the story (just because that's what your boss or client wants to say). Say something interesting.

By wisely, I mean get your message across in a more subtle manner, making sure the words back up, reinforce, reiterate or introduce a key message.

For those unfamiliar with 'key messages' these are the 'basic truths' of a situation or organisation that sum up your stance and the facts as you see it. Key messages for a business should be written in stone but constantly checked and updated.

There is not enough room in this book to cover key messages, which are unique to an organisation. They should be carefully thought through and in harmony with your communications strategy.

The best way to show you how you can incorporate key messages into your media release via your quote is to show you some media releases I have written for clients. Only the names have been changed to protect the innocent…

Media Release

Sunny-side-up Marketing Board

Calling all Bread Bakers, Cheese Makers and Food Creators

Growers and food producers are being asked to step out from the shadows and help give the Sunny-side-up Region a whole new food identity and culture.

It is no secret the region wants a farmer's market, with more than 400 survey forms already completed in support of one.

Now, organisers need growers and food producers to step forward and show their interest, so plans can move forward.

Already, 40 food producers have expressed interest but project manager Apple Blossom, from the Sunny-side-up Marketing Board, knows there are many more out there that could reap the benefits of a regular farmer's market in the region.

"We have been overwhelmed with the response to our survey asking people for their thoughts on a farmer's market," she said.

"Now, we need to start the process moving forward with solid commitment from growers and food producers. Importantly, we need them to also complete a survey form, as their thoughts on where, how often, what day and what time a farmer's market should take place are obviously of utmost importance."

Notice how the quotes back up and reinforce what has been said earlier in the story. Do not go off on a tangent. Your media release should have one or two central themes, which, in this case, are a 'call to arms' for more growers and food producers while also reinforcing the need for a market (as evidenced by the 'overwhelming response' to the survey).

Notice how the quote makes organisers appear focused on delivering – they are not messing around.

Your quotation is an opportunity to not only communicate a key message or two but to also add colour and life to your story. And that is what a media release is – a story – whether it's about a new CEO, product or factory – you are telling a story.

If you have a choice of quotes from your spokesperson, choose one of the most colourful quotes (this is your chance to add some personality) while also being mindful of your key messages and the overall thrust of the release.

Your quote also lets the reader know there is someone behind the story who knows what they are talking about (remember how we talked about relevance).

Your spokesperson should be someone in "authority" and who has experience in that field (experience can be real and long-term or it can be learned in a matter of minutes through diligent research).

Your spokesperson can be your chairman, managing director, the business owner (sometimes this is mum or dad), the supervisor, senior volunteer, chief engineer or head researcher etc. depending on the topic or issue.

If you are a communications professional you will no doubt have a 'stable' of spokespeople, trained and ready to deliver relevant, pithy quotations on a range of topics related to their field and/or whatever area of the organisation is under the media spotlight.

A note here to readers. I was delivering a workshop a few years ago and one of the participants was shocked to find out that not all "quotes" have actually come out of the mouth of the person quoted.

Allow me to explain. If you are a communications professional you could be writing as many as two or three media releases a day – maybe more. You cannot always reach your senior management. It is quite normal to have a collection of pre-approved quotes to choose from, depending what the release is about. Think of it as a 'pick and mix'.

Alternatively, you, as a communications technician who fully understands the organisation, will "make up" the quotes based on knowledge of the issue and then get the media release approved – preferably by the person quoted but if she/he is not available, a trusted and authorised deputy.

In this way, it is quite legitimate to say 'he said' or 'she said' after the direct quote.

Of course, not all quotes are created like this – it is also quite 'normal' for the communications professional to speak directly with a senior manager, ask them a few pertinent questions on the issue and create the media release from that conversation. But it is not always so.

TOP TIP	Never distribute a release with a quotation in it without approval of those words from the person to whom those words are attributed (unless you are very, very sure of yourself and/or it is a crisis situation demanding speed and, even then, I would seek some kind of approval from a senior person in the organisation – unless you are that person).

Paragraph Six

Paragraph six is also devoted to your quotation (as in the previous example). More colour, more information, reinforce your view.

One paragraph is rarely enough to get your whole message across so why not go for another paragraph while you are at it? The journalist could well chop it out of the story but it's worth a try.

This is also why your quote should be vibrant and interesting (not all subject matter lends itself to this, of course, but you can still try and be as interesting as possible, even with 'dry' topics).

Being interesting does not have to mean being sensationalist (in fact it should not mean this) but do try and use strong, punchy words where you can.

Putting the facts across, succinctly and accurately, is interesting for the reader.

If you have got them as far as paragraph six, they must be at least somewhat interested in the story/topic.

On the following page is an example of making quotes work for you in a media release.

> **TOP TIP** Do not use quotations for gratuitous sales messages and irrelevant detail. Make them work for you. Back up your story and reinforce the angle of the release. Include 'on topic' key messages.

Whitsunday Marine Academy featured on TV's Get-away-from-it-all

The joys of sailing in the Whitsundays will be beamed to 10 million people on Channel 12's Get-away-from-it-all program this Thursday (October 14).

The Getaway-from-it-all crew and presenter Kenny Lawdry joined the Whitsunday Marine Academy on a jaunt around the Whitsunday Islands, which will be aired as part of a feature on 'The 10 best things to do in Australia'.

The Whitsunday Marine Academy is a locally owned and run business that teaches potential sailors recreational sailing skills for career or personal use. It is hoped the TV exposure will boost the region's marine tourism industry.

The academy's Matt Bradley said it had been a fantastic experience, with Kenny Lawdry very happy to be 'shown the ropes' by the crew.

"Kenny really enjoyed the experience and was very enthusiastic about sailing around the Whitsundays and seeing all of our beautiful islands," he said.

"The crew were more than pleased to have an extra deckhand on board and Kenny really got involved in everything, from hoisting the sails to steering and look-out duties."

Notice how the quote (paragraphs five and six) brings it alive – you can picture Kenny jumping all over the boat with the beautiful Whitsunday Islands as a backdrop (key message = promoting the islands).

As the reader, I can feel the sun on my back as I hoist the sails alongside Kenny… great promotion for the region's marine tourism industry.

How much speech?

I would suggest two to three paragraphs (maximum) of direct speech for the average media release and if your interviewee or spokesperson has a lot to say on the matter, you can then go into indirect speech in the next paragraph (or two – but only if it is interesting/relevant).

You can also introduce a second spokesperson but be sure to clearly identify the two as separate spokespeople (name and title) and make sure it is very clear which one is speaking.

Only very complex issues, in my opinion, would warrant a third spokesperson and even then, it might be better to give the journalist the crux of the story (300 words) and invite him or her to conduct an interview with one of your spokespeople if the story interests them.

Note: Journalists do, quite often, call the source of the media release for more information and quotes if they are interested in the story (or they call the contact person at the end of the release). This is a way that the journalist and publication can differentiate their story from all the other publications that have received the same release. Quite often, another comment made by the spokesperson can spark a completely different angle (which is great for the reporter but a lesson in being cautious and staying 'on message' for the spokesperson).

TOP TIP	Direct interviews with a journalist are always great and they are especially useful if it is a technical or complex issue. Be sure to have some fact sheets and/or background information on hand to assist the journalist.

Paragraph Seven

This can also be your quote – either direct speech or indirect speech (see Top Tip on page 28 for the difference).

As mentioned, for an 'average' media release I would suggest no more than three paragraphs of quotation and whether you use direct or indirect speech is really a matter of style (although I would suggest at least one paragraph of direct speech to bring the story to life – it is more immediate, more 'now').

Before we leave the quotation, some other quick pointers:

Always identify your spokesperson by their full name and title the first time they are mentioned ie. Mr Richard Jones, CEO of Jones & Co Lawyers, said…

Thereafter, you can just refer to him as Mr Jones. You should ask a female whether she would like to be quoted as Mrs or Ms.

Always try and name your spokesperson if possible (don't just say 'a spokesperson said…') as names add personality, engagement, transparency and authority. 'Spokesperson' is so anonymous (although I do accept sometimes it is necessary to use this).

As already mentioned, misspelling names is a sin. There is no excuse for it.

Whether you say '...said Mr Jones' or '...Mr Jones said' at the end of your direct quote is a matter of style and can vary between newspapers (check which one your target uses). Some newspapers start with 'Mr Jones said...' and then go into the quotation.

An example of using your seventh paragraph for quotation (three paragraphs of quotation in total) follows in this fun example:

Birthday bonanza continues unabated: More than a third off selected sailing holidays.

Sunny Yacht Charters' 35th birthday promotion continues to dazzle holidaymakers with its massive 35 per cent off selected boats and dates.

The world's leading sailing holiday company turns 35 this year and to celebrate, it is giving customers a whopping 35 percent off selected last-minute bookings from their base in the Whitsundays, north Queensland.

Hundreds of holidaymakers happy to take their holiday at short notice have already benefited from this extraordinary deal and now Sunny Yacht Charters is releasing dates for October and November.

And this is in addition to Sunny's other 35th birthday promotion where customers can get $35 cash back simply by saying 'Happy Birthday Sunny's' when they book.

"We have been overwhelmed by the response to our birthday promotion," said Sunny's marketing manager Kim Letterman.

"October and November in the Whitsundays are absolutely beautiful and holidaymakers can really take time to explore this magical aquatic wonderland at their leisure with these great deals.

"With some really low airfares at the moment, cruising the beautiful Whitsundays has never looked so good."

These three short, sharp paragraphs of direct speech paint a picture of the beautiful Whitsundays and give readers a reason to go there.

The quote also says the response to the promotion has been overwhelming, implying other people have 'bought into it' (ooh, it must be good…).

Paragraphs Eight and Nine

This is where you add more detail to your story, provide more information for the reader and offer 'substantiating evidence' to back up your earlier claims.

It is also a great opportunity to include some more key messages.

The trick is to remain relevant. Back up what you have already said. Stay on topic. Round out the story for the reader.

Hence, with the previous media release example about the farmer's market, I use paragraphs seven, eight and nine to say...

7   *Ms Blossom said people not currently making a product but who would like to, should register their interest, as a farmer's market acted as a catalyst for food production in a region.*

8   *"If the market is going to be sustainable, we need a diverse range of products to offer buyers and we would like to hear from anyone who creates – or has thought about creating – a food product, including cheese makers and bread makers."*

9   *Ms Blossom said the Sunny-side-up Marketing Board could help people develop their food ideas into actual marketable products.*

Notice how in this case, the eighth paragraph is also a quote. This is perfectly allowable, as long as it is interesting, informative and on message.

Remember how we said this release had two major themes – a 'call to arms' for more growers and food producers, while also reinforcing the need for a market – these paragraphs continue both these themes.

Organisers are actually offering to help food producers so they can sell their product at the farmer's market, which means a more diverse range of stalls, which is better for visitors.

And in our earlier example about the Whitsunday Marine Academy, paragraphs seven, eight and nine went like this...

7   *Business manager at Enterprise Whitsundays Mary Ward said it was fantastic exposure for a small local business to be featured on a popular show like Getaway-from-it-all – which has an international audience of 10 million viewers a week – and this would hopefully boost the region's marine tourism industry.*

8   *"The Whitsunday Marine Academy offers visitors, of all ages, the opportunity to learn to sail or develop skills that could allow them to crew or skipper Super Yachts in some of the world's most exotic sailing destinations," she said.*

9   *"We hope that by being featured on the show this week, travellers with a working holiday visa might see the Whitsundays as a place to start a career in marine tourism."*

As in the previous example, the paragraphs have been used for quotation but they also add further detail and information, which is the 'job' of these paragraphs.

They also need to back up what has been said earlier in the story. Mary Ward – who we understand to be 'qualified' to speak, as she is business manager at Enterprise Whitsundays (the name denotes some kind of economic development role) – backs up what was said in paragraph three, namely, it is hoped the TV exposure will boost the region's marine tourism industry.

Some other points to note for these later but still important paragraphs are:

If you find yourself wandering off topic, jot down some notes and save it for another day. If you have that much to say, you probably have another media release (remember, only one or two themes per release).

A media release should really be about one main issue or topic – there should be a news angle of some kind. It is not an excuse to regale the reader with everything you know about your organisation (if you do, it will get chopped or binned).

Readers (and journalists) are interested in stories – stories have a beginning, a middle and an end. And a purpose.

TOP TIP	When it is reported speech, it should be 'would' not 'will', as in...Business manager at Enterprise Whitsundays Mary Ward said it was fantastic exposure for a small local business to be featured on a popular show like Getaway-from-it-all...and this <u>would</u> hopefully boost the region's marine tourism industry.

Paragraph Ten

Although it is the last paragraph of your 10-Paragraph Press Release©, the tenth paragraph is nevertheless important.

This is your 'wrap-up'. Depending what your release is about, this could be...

- For more information contact...

- A meeting has been scheduled to discuss the findings...

- A motion has been tabled and will be discussed at the AGM next week...

- The company is awaiting a report and will publish the results in...

- An investigation is being carried out with the results known some-time next year...

When it is 'softer' news, the tenth paragraph can even be humorous.

From the examples we looked at above, our tenth paragraphs are as follows:

For more information about the farmer's market, or to register your interest as a stallholder or food producer, contact Apple Blossom at Sunny-side-up Marketing Board on 5555 5555 or email: apple@sunnysideup.com.au.

Sometimes media releases contain a call-to-action in the last paragraph.

Journalists and editors do not mind this if it is a not-for-profit or charity, a council acting in the community's interest or some other such organisation that is ultimately serving its readers (a museum or economic development agency, for example).

Where there is a commercial transaction suggested, the journalist will more often than not chop it out (unless, as stated, it is a travel story where deals are often included).

So in our previous example about sailing holidays, our tenth paragraph is a little more blatant…

For up-to-date information on Sunny's 35th birthday offer of a 35 per cent discount off selected boats and dates – including the current available timeslots in October and November – check the special offers page on the website: www.sunny.com.au. For more information or reservations call 1800 555 555 or email sunny@sunny.com.au

Quite often, the tenth or last paragraph is some kind of 'pay off', as in the media release about the Whitsunday Marine Academy appearing on TV…

Viewers will be able to phone or email the program immediately after the feature to make a booking for the sail training. For more information on sail training in the Whitsundays visit: www.whitsundaysailtraining.com

We have already told the reader what date the show is airing in the first paragraph so this kind of completes the circle for the reader.

It also lets the reader know where they can learn to sail…like Kenny Lawdry… Celebrity endorsement, by the way, is very powerful in media releases, if it is appropriate and relevant.

The 10-Paragraph Press Release© Complete

Following is a complete media release that demonstrates the whole 10-Paragraph Press Release© process.

Whitsunday Community Bank a step closer

Whitsunday residents are one step closer to having their very own bank, which would fund projects in the region.

A committee has been formed to steer the Whitsunday Community Bank, which is still at concept stage but, if successful, could see millions of dollars kept in the local community.

This money would be used to fund further investment and future jobs.

The committee – including residents, business people and former councillors – is calling for pledges of support for the bank from the local community.

"A number of key people from across the region are committed to making this a possibility by establishing a steering group for the Whitsunday Community Bank," said committee chairman Rebecca Ronald.

"At the moment we are collecting pledges and we need at least 300 residents to pledge their support for the project.

"A pledge is an indication of your intention to purchase shares in the Whitsunday Community Bank. You are not required to contribute any money at this time, it is simply an indication of your support."

Ms Ronald said a community bank would encourage collaboration on, and commitment to, major projects in the area, benefiting everyone.

It would also keep local money and jobs in the community, which was good for everyone, whether currently working, or still at school and wanting to stay living and working in the region.

For a leaflet explaining more about the Whitsunday Community Bank project and a list of committee members, call Ms Ronald on 5555 5555.

ends

Notice how the crux of the story is summarised in the first three paragraphs:

1 *Whitsunday residents are one step closer to having their very own bank, which would fund projects in the region.*

The first paragraph contains the Who (Whitsunday residents) and the What (they are one step closer to having their very own bank).

The second paragraph then goes on to expand on this:

2 *A committee has been formed to steer the Whitsunday Community Bank, which is still at concept stage but, if successful, could see millions of dollars kept in the local community.*

The second paragraph gives us the full name of the bank, advises the reader it is still at concept stage (this is a kind of When – it is not ready to go yet but it's getting there) and what the outcome could be.

The third paragraph then tells us, specifically, what these millions of dollars would be used for in the local community and gives us our Why (Why do we need this bank?)...

3   This money would be used to fund further investment and future jobs.

Paragraph four then acts as a bridging paragraph.

4   The committee – including residents, business people and former coun-cillors – is calling for pledges of support for the bank from the local community.

We are "introduced" to the committee (it is no surprise when the next paragraph is a quote from the committee chairman) and the paragraph 'throws the story forward' (they are calling for pledges of support).

Paragraphs five, six and seven are the quotation.

5   "A number of key people from across the region are committed to making this a possibility by establishing a steering group for the Whitsunday Community Bank," said committee chairman Rebecca Ronald.

6   "At the moment we are collecting pledges and we need at least 300 residents to pledge their support for the project.

7   "A pledge is an indication of your intention to purchase shares in the Whitsunday Community Bank. You are not required to contribute any money at this time, it is simply an indication of your support."

The quotes back up paragraph four (where we have already been told the committee is calling for pledges of support) and explains more about what a pledge is, while allaying people's fears of having to hand over money now and communicating the strength and solidarity of the bank thus far ("A number of key people from across the region are committed to making this a possibility by establishing a steering group...").

The overall thrust or theme is clearly a call for pledges but supporting messages are also included.

Paragraphs eight and nine add more detail and information.

8   *Ms Ronald said a community bank would encourage collaboration on, and commitment to, major projects in the area, benefiting everyone.*

9   *It would also keep local money and jobs in the community, which was good for everyone, whether currently working, or still at school and wanting to stay living and working in the region.*

Paragraph eight is an indirect quote from Ms Ronald and expands on the secondary 'benefits for everyone' theme.

Paragraph nine expands and builds on paragraph three, where 'future jobs' were first mentioned. More detail is given about who would benefit from these jobs (current workers and school students).

Paragraph 10 is the wrap-up, advising the reader where they can obtain more information about both the bank and the committee, if they are interested.

10   *For a leaflet explaining more about the Whitsunday Community Bank project and a list of committee members, call Ms Ronald on 5555 5555.*

TOP TIP — If you do have a lot more information that is pertinent to your story, do not try and cram it into your release, rather, use a tactic such as Editor's Notes, Fact Sheets, Backgrounders and Media Kits to communicate additional information to the journalist. See Bonus Section for more information.

Conclusion

So there you have it, the 10-Paragraph Press Release©.

The wonderful thing about writing is that everyone writes slightly differently – if you gave 10 journalists a brief for the same story, they would all deliver something slightly different.

But there are universal rules for writing that you can follow to give your release the best chance of being read by the journalist and therefore published.

Journalists write like they do for a reason – many reasons, in fact – but probably top of the list is readability.

In this book, I have taken you through the basic steps of writing like a journalist, so your media releases are noticed, picked up and used.

Following is a two-page summary of the 10-Paragraph Press Release© to act as a handy check list.

The 10-Paragraph Press Release© Check List

Paragraph One

The most important paragraph – it must grab the reader's attention, be short and pithy while summing up the crux of the story.

Paragraph Two

Clarifies or expands on the first paragraph. Begins to set the story up. Will include as many of the five Ws and one H as the story dictates and the paragraph can take.

Paragraph Three

This is the swinger – either reinforcing paragraph two and adding more Ws or setting up the conflict ie. this has happened but now this has happened (and it's an issue…).

Paragraph three should complete your summary of the story (the whole story should be summarised in three paragraphs). If the story is cut, it stands alone.

Paragraph Four

The bridge. You have summarised your story, now you start to take your reader on a journey. Set up your spokesperson either with an introductory statement (linking to main thrust of story) or an indirect quote.

Paragraph Five

Your quote. Adds colour and personality but also your chance to get your side of the story across.

Must be accurate and honest. Can use quote to include key messages.

Paragraph Six

Continue quote. Make it work for you. Make it interesting.

Back up or reinforce what has gone before while also adding a new fact or two to keep the reader's interest.

Paragraph Seven

Either more direct quotation (depending how verbose your spokesperson is) or move to indirect quote to start to wrap it up; or jump straight into more info…

Paragraph Eight

More information, facts, detail. But stay on topic. It is all about backing up what has gone before.

One release = one angle (or major thrust).

Facts and information must be relevant. Chance to include more key messages but don't overdo them (stay on track).

Paragraph Nine

Start to wrap up your story. Another key message, perhaps, or one more pertinent fact to flesh out the story (if you're good, it will be both). Remember you can use direct or indirect quotes here as well if appropriate and introduce a second spokesperson if required.

Paragraph Ten

The wrap-up. What is the conclusion or next step? Don't leave your reader hanging. Give them something, even if it is the promise of something happening in the future (a meeting will take place…a white paper will be published…a vote will be held…).

Sending Your Release

I am not going to go into targeting your release in this book, which is more about the actual crafting of your media release.

Targeting is one of the Holy Grails of communication. Yes, we all know it would be lovely to give our client – or our own business - a big spread in a glossy magazine but which one and when? What type of story should I pitch and for which section…and to whom?

It is what keeps communication professionals awake at night.

But as a former journalist, I will just offer you a few pointers on sending your release, as this can be extremely important in the 'kill or be killed' world of newsrooms (and I have checked these pointers out with a few current journalists).

Deadlines, deadlines, deadlines…it is the "location, location, location" of the media world and cannot be over stressed. Meeting them, that is.

Meeting deadlines is what drives a journalist's day and if you do not fit in with these, you will greatly diminish your chances of being published (and also of having a reasonable relationship with the journalist).

Know your publications and their deadlines and remember, there will be different deadlines for different sections of the paper or magazine. Broadcast media (radio and TV) will have different deadlines again (as will online news and entertainment).

Email is the format favoured by journalists nowadays, preferably with the release embedded into the email. If you must attach a document, make sure it is not a large file size and that it is in a format that the journalist can easily cut and paste from (Word is great).

The issue of whether you send journalists logos, product images, mastheads, info-graphics, audio files, videos and anything else that takes up space in their email inbox, is an interesting one.

Some journalists can have upwards of 100 emails a day (25-50 is normal) and large files run the risk of serious computer overload. Not to mention brain overload.

However, the flip-side is, a lot of 'traditional' media outlets such as newspapers have corresponding websites and therefore welcome additional, more visual, information (a lot of stories nowadays go straight to web).

I think the answer is to ask the journalist what his or her preference is, which reiterates the need to have solid relationships with your media contacts.

And don't forget, you can also create a media room, or media centre, on your website, with product images, logos, brochures, past media releases, audio and video etc. that can be easily accessed by journalists when they need them.

In terms of following up with the journalist once you have sent your release, it really does depend on the journalist and the publication.

Bear in mind these words from a busy newspaper journalist: "In my experience, there is a fine line between the squeaky wheel getting the most oil and annoying the journalist to the point where they don't want to answer the media release writer's emails or phone calls."

Pictures paint a thousand words

Sending pictures to print journalists is tricky as they have differing opinions but if you can get a photo published alongside your story you have instantly doubled your coverage (but remember, not all stories lend themselves to a picture).

Some journalists prefer you to send two or three low resolution samples and they can then request a high resolution version of a particular image. Others prefer you to send something they can use straightaway ie. a good, high resolution image (minimum 1mb but no more than about 4mb).

This is why you need to build robust relationships with journalists and find out exactly what their needs and wants are. What journalists do seem to agree on is not embedding pictures into the email itself as this can create problems, especially when transitioning between systems eg. Mac to PC.

Include some kind of action in your photo, even if it is two people shaking hands or someone handing something to the other person (that's preferable to them standing there doing absolutely nothing).

Static shots are 'bad' - this is why you see photos of people climbing stairs or seemingly walking along (they might actually be stationary but will be posed as if they are walking to add 'movement' to the photo).

Sunglasses hiding people's faces are a no-no (unless your subjects are on a yacht or similar) and beware boldly patterned scarves, hats, caps etc. that steal the focus away from the face. And don't waste the journalist's time with "pin" heads, shadows on faces, trees coming out of people's heads and photos that are out of focus.

Include a clear, concise caption at the end of your release summing up the photo and providing everyone's name (first and second name and, if relevant, their title/job description). These must be spelt correctly and convention dictates that you provide names from left to right.

Online Media Releases

The internet has changed everything and now you can send your media release out to potential customers and clients directly via the worldwide web.

Traditional media are still as important as they have always been, and have themselves harnessed the power of the web to both find stories and information, and put their own stories and opinions out there.

But in addition to utilising traditional media to tell your story, there is an opportunity for public relations practitioners and business owners to also harness that power and send their news direct-to-consumer via the internet.

Media releases for online distribution should be written in much the same way as those sent to traditional media outlets. The format (as explained in this book) is the same.

However, because your media release is competing with literally millions of other pieces of communication on the internet, you need to give the search engines a bit of a hand to find yours, and you do this through keywords.

Keywords are king

Keywords are, quite simply, the words people type into search engines to find something they are interested in, whether this is an organisation, product, person, topic, issue, event or anything at all they require information about.

So in its simplest form, you can 'optimise' your media release for distribution on the net by including plenty of keywords, giving it the best chance of being found online.

The way search engines work, they will give more 'weight' to the header and first couple of paragraphs than they will to the rest of the media release, so make sure you include as many keywords in your header and first few paragraphs as you can, without bogging down the story.

To revert to the example about the Sunny-side-up Marketing Board's call for farmer's market participants (keywords in bold):

*Calling all Bread Bakers, Cheese Makers and **Food Creators***

***Growers** and **food producers** are being asked to step out from the shadows and help give the **Sunny-side-up Region** a whole new **food identity** and **culture**.*

*It is no secret the region wants a **farmer's market**, with more than 400 survey forms already completed in support of one.*

*Now, organisers need **growers and food producers** to step forward and show their interest, so plans can move forward.*

*Already, 40 **food producers** have expressed interest but project manager Apple Blossom, from the **Sunny-side-up Marketing Board**, knows there are many more out there that could reap the benefits of a regular **farmer's market** in the region.*

Notice how the words **food producers** and **food creators** are mentioned four times in the header and first four paragraphs of the release. This was one of the main themes of the release – a call for food producers to come forward. The word **growers** is also in the first and third paragraphs.

The words **farmer's market** are mentioned twice – for people searching for 'farmer's markets' – and the mention of the **Sunny-side-up Region** and **Sunny-side-up Marketing Board** in the first few paragraphs will tie the search to the Sunny-side-up Region (for those who have entered this as a search term).

The words **food identity** and **culture** are also in the first paragraph as this is a very popular theme with people who like visiting farmer's markets.

More is more

With online media releases you can really 'go to town' and attach images, logos, audio files, video files, PDFs and podcasts – in fact, any multi-media files you think will add to and enhance your story. The online world is a multi-faceted one, hungry for news in many formats.

Links

Include anchor text and hyperlinks in your online media release to point readers back to your website. Ideally, create separate landing pages on your site for distinct target audiences and/or offers. Ensure the landing pages are relevant to the release to continue the momentum and guide your customer through the sales/donation/subscription process (or whatever you want them to do).

You can also add hashtags to online media releases so they can be found by people looking for specific topics online.

> **TOP TIP** Do not stuff so many keywords into your release that it fails to read properly and therefore engage your reader. Readability is paramount. If you are following the rules of the 10-Paragraph Press Release© then your release will be chock-full of keywords anyway, based on the rules of relevance and putting your most interesting/salient facts first.

And lastly...

Do not litter your release with CAPITALS, **bold**, *italics*, colours, BIG writing and underlining – it is very annoying. The first thing the journalist will do is remove it all, so he or she can work with basic text.

If you must highlight something, use either bold or italics (but not both) and use very sparingly.

Bullet points are acceptable if you really do have a list of things that are better communicated in a list (and in those instances, journalists like bullet points).

Always date your release (you'd be surprised how many people don't) and if you use a 'tomorrow', 'yesterday' or 'next week', assist the journalist by putting the precise date in brackets after it.

Add a catchy headline. Chances are it will be changed (subeditors and editors like to come up with their own headlines to suit the story/page/feature) but it will at least catch the journalist's eye.

Make your header relevant to the topic while also being impactful and interesting (a tall order, I know, in 10-15 words).

And while we're talking about impact, don't just put 'press release' in the subject box of your email. That means nothing to the busy journalist. If your headline is short and punchy, use that, or use a chopped down version of your headline. Whatever happens, use your imagination.

And lastly, do not forget to put a contact name and phone number (and email address), should the journalist need further information or clarification.

Who you put at the bottom of the release for further comment or interview will depend on the nature of the release (ie. the relevant expert or voice of authority). If it is non technical or specialised, it would normally be the communications person. If technical/specialised, try and put someone who can realistically assist the journalist.

I would suggest also putting your name and number, as the media contact and author of the release.

Good luck and remember, never give up – practice makes perfect.

Getting your message out there takes time and patience and your first few media releases might not get taken up but you will improve over time.

Happy writing.

Deborah A. L. Friend.

P.S. The other press releases used as examples are following, so you can read them in their entirety if you wish. Otherwise, skip straight to the Bonus Section.

Media Release

Sunny-side-up Marketing Board

Calling all Bread Bakers, Cheese Makers and Food Creators

Growers and food producers are being asked to step out from the shadows and help give the Sunny-side-up Region a whole new food identity and culture.

It is no secret the region wants a farmer's market, with more than 400 survey forms already completed in support of one.

Now, organisers need growers and food producers to step forward and show their interest, so plans can move forward.

Already, 40 food producers have expressed interest but project manager Apple Blossom, from the Sunny-side-up Marketing Board, knows there are many more out there that could reap the benefits of a regular farmer's market in the region.

"We have been overwhelmed with the response to our survey asking people for their thoughts on a farmer's market," she said.

"Now, we need to start the process moving forward with solid commitment from growers and food producers. Importantly, we need them to also complete a survey form, as their thoughts on where, how often, what day and what time a farmer's market should take place are obviously of utmost importance."

Ms Blossom said people not currently making a product but who would like to, should register their interest, as a farmer's market acted as a catalyst for food production in a region.

"If the market is going to be sustainable, we need a diverse range of products to offer buyers and we would like to hear from anyone who creates – or has thought about creating – a food product, including cheese makers and bread makers."

Ms Blossom said the Sunny-side-up Marketing Board could help people develop their food ideas into actual marketable products.

For more information about the farmer's market, or to register your interest as a stallholder or food producer, contact Apple Blossom at Sunny-side-up Marketing Board on 5555 5555 or email: apple@ sunnysideup.com.au.

Ends

For more information about this media release please contact the Sunny-side-up Marketing Board's media executive on…

Media Release

Whitsunday Marine Academy

Whitsunday Marine Academy featured on TV's Getaway-from-it-all

The joys of sailing in the Whitsundays will be beamed to 10 million people on Channel 12's Getaway-from-it-all program this Thursday (October 14).

The Getaway-from-it-all crew and presenter Kenny Lawdry joined the Whitsunday Marine Academy on a jaunt around the Whitsunday Islands, which will be aired as part of a feature on 'The 10 best things to do in Australia'.

The Whitsunday Marine Academy is a locally owned and run business that teaches potential sailors recreational sailing skills for career or personal use. It is hoped the TV exposure will boost the region's marine tourism industry.

The academy's Matt Bradley said it had been a fantastic experience, with Kenny Lawdry very happy to be 'shown the ropes' by the crew.

"Kenny really enjoyed the experience and was very enthusiastic about sailing around the Whitsundays and seeing all of our beautiful islands," he said.

"The crew were more than pleased to have an extra deckhand on board and Kenny really got involved in everything from hoisting the sails to steering and look-out duties."

Business manager at Enterprise Whitsundays Mary Ward said it was fantastic exposure for a small local business to be featured on a popular show like Getaway-from-it-all – which has an international audience of 10 million viewers a week – and this would hopefully boost the region's marine tourism industry.

"The Whitsunday Marine Academy offers visitors, of all ages, the opportunity to learn to sail or develop skills that could allow them to crew or skipper Super Yachts in some of the world's most exotic sailing destinations," she said.

"We hope that by being featured on the show this week, travellers with a working holiday visa might see the Whitsundays as a place to start a career in marine tourism."

Viewers will be able to phone or email the program immediately after the feature to make a booking for the sail training. For more information on sail training in the Whitsundays visit: www.whitsundaysailtraining.com

Media Release

Sunny Yacht Charters

Birthday bonanza continues unabated: More than a third off selected sailing holidays.

Sunny Yacht Charters' 35th birthday promotion continues to dazzle holidaymakers with its massive 35 per cent off selected boats and dates.

The world's leading sailing holiday company turns 35 this year and to celebrate, it is giving customers a whopping 35 per cent off selected last-minute bookings from their base in the Whitsundays, north Queensland.

Hundreds of holidaymakers happy to take their holiday at short notice have already benefited from this extraordinary deal and now Sunny Yacht Charters is releasing dates for October and November.

And this is *in addition* to Sunny's other 35th birthday promotion where customers can get $35 cash back simply by saying 'Happy Birthday Sunny' when they book.

"We have been overwhelmed by the response to our birthday promotion," said Sunny's marketing manager Kim Letterman.

"October and November in the Whitsundays are absolutely beautiful and holidaymakers can really take time to explore this magical aquatic wonderland at their leisure with these great deals.

"With some really low airfares at the moment, cruising the beautiful Whitsundays has never looked so good."

Established in 1974 in Europe, Sunny grew rapidly in the 1980s and 1990s and now has 29 bases in 20 countries including the Mediterranean, the Caribbean, Thailand, Australia, New Zealand the Seychelles, Tonga, Croatia, Malaysia, Cuba, Tahiti and Corsica.

Today, Sunny Yacht Charters offers boat charter holidays, sailing flotillas, regatta participation, corporate and team-building events and sailing schools.

For up-to-date information on Sunny's 35th birthday offer of a 35 per cent discount off selected boats and dates – including the current available time slots in October and November – check the special offers page on the website: www.sunny.com.au.

For more information or reservations call 1800 555 555 or email sunny@sunny.com.au.

BONUS SECTION

News Values

"News is what people are talking about."

The basic news values have not changed in centuries but I believe more news values have been added as our news, and the way we consume it, have changed over the years.

I have therefore provided a list of what are widely considered to be the "traditional" news values and then I have added a few topics of my own to reflect the modern news agenda, including 'shock factor', where something is news simply because it is shocking.

It is not an exhaustive list, and some people might not agree with every news value I have included - if you search 'news values' online you will see there has been a lot written about news values over the years.

But the list will give you a very good start to understanding 'what is news?'.

Again, practice makes perfect, so take the time to trawl through newspapers (traditional and online) and news-style magazines and identify the news values in stories using this list as a reference.

One news story can, and often does, contain several news values.

"Traditional" News Values

Celebration	Heroism	Royals
Celebrity or notable	Human interest	Scandal
Conflict	Humour	Sex
Danger	Impact (on people)	Sport
Death	Money	Timeliness
Disaster	Mystery	Underdog
Emotion	Novelty (unusual)	Victim
Frequency	Pain	
Hardship	Proximity	

Newsworthy Topics

In addition to the above, the following topics are very newsworthy and will appear again and again in news coverage all over the world.

You will find that most of them relate to the news value of 'impact' – all the topics listed below impact on us as humans in our everyday lives.

Again, it is not exhaustive but it should act as a handy check list of what constitutes news nowadays.

Careers	Drugs	Housing
Children	Education	Jobs
Consumerism	Environment	New technologies
Cute animals	Health	Shock factor

Note: Stories about these topics would also contain "traditional" news values, for example, a story about jobs could contain:

- Conflict (employees striking or picketing)

- Hardship (employees losing their jobs)

- Scandal (if there had been a cover-up to do with job losses)

- Proximity (if it is a local news bulletin)

Have a look through the weekend paper and you will find lots of features and stories about careers, homes, schools, health issues and the environment.

When you are creating 'news' for your client or your own business, it is about aligning your news with what is already out there.

Jump on the band wagon…or take the current media discussion in a different direction.

And follow what's trending on social media - a very good indication of what people are "talking about".

Tight Writing

Brevity is everything in writing…less is more.

Also known as concise writing, or 'tight' writing by journalists, it is a combination of short sentences and short, simple words. It is about being economical with words (not verbose).

Below is just a sample of simpler, shorter words that can be used in place of longer words but there are plenty more.

Don't say...	Do say...	Don't say...	Do say...
A percentage of	some	Demonstrate	show
Accordingly	so	Despite the fact that	although
Adjacent to	next to, near	Discontinue	stop
Ahead of schedule	early	Endeavour	try
Approximately	about	In addition	also
Ascertain	learn	In attendance	there, present
Assistance	help	Large proportion of	many
Attempt	try	Manufacture	make
Behind schedule	late	Merchandise	goods
Beverage	drink	Prior to	before
By way of...	through	Retail outlets	shops
Commence	start, begin	Subsequently	later
Concerning	about	Sufficient	enough
Constructed	made, built	Terminate	end
Currently	now	With reference to	about

When you are doing your research into how journalists write their stories also check out the language they use (and the length of their sentences).

Additional Information for Journalists

If you do have a lot of information that is pertinent to your story, do not try and cram it into the release, which should be a story about a specific happening or issue, with an angle.

To communicate additional information to the journalist use one of the following:

Editor's Notes

This is key messages and information about your organisation that you attach at the end of your release.

This allows the journalist to pick out salient facts, figures etc. that he or she feels will enhance the story (or if they don't actually use them in the story, it broadens their knowledge of your organisation).

Editor's Notes shouldn't really change much as they are basic truths about your organisation but they should be regularly checked and updated when necessary (eg. Number of employees, name of CEO, head office location etc.).

So, in the case of Sunny Yacht Charters, the Editor's Notes might look like this:

- Sunny Yacht Charters' Australian base is located in the Whitsunday Islands, Queensland.

- Flights arrive every day from major cities, with the Sunny Yacht Charters base just three minutes from the airport in the air-conditioned courtesy bus.

- Guests can be on their boat and sailing out the marina within a couple of hours, following their safety briefing.

- Sunny Yacht Charters can even provision the boat for guests, saving yet more time.

- The fleet of high-specification luxury yachts and catamarans cater for every kind of sailing experience and holiday.

- Yachts can be hired with or without a skipper.

- Guests' comfort is as important as the safety and performance of the yachts, which are built to Sunny Yacht Charters' exacting standards in conjunction with the world's top yacht designers.

Fact Sheets

As the name implies, these are facts on issues and topics that might assist with the story. So, for example, if you were doing a release about a dangerous stretch of highway, you might include a Fact Sheet with statistics about the highway including accident rates, number of kilometres requiring flood proofing, money committed to improvements by various governments etc.

Fact Sheets are useful when there is some detail involved but you don't want to bog the story down.

So, a media release announcing a new wine might also have a Fact Sheet available about vintages, grape varieties, growing times, weather, temperature etc. for journalists in this field.

Backgrounders

Pretty much similar to the above but they might have more background to an issue such as examples of previous newspaper coverage on the topic, where to find more information (eg. useful websites).

A chronological timeline with milestones is helpful if it is an ongoing issue or project.

The name of the game is to assist journalists.

Media Kits

These are the full package and can include a current media release (what's happening now?), previous media releases, information about key personnel (often called bios or profiles), detailed product information (maybe the company brochure), Fact Sheets, Backgrounders and contact details. But be selective - think about what each journalist needs (don't just throw a whole load of information at them).

Media kits can be digital or in hard-copy format and, of course, digital media kits can include podcasts, videos, audio etc.

Thank you for reading this book. If you have any questions or queries please email me at: questions@writeawaywhitsundays.com.au

Deborah A.L. Friend.

www.ingramcontent.com/pod-product-compliance
Lightning Source LLC
Chambersburg PA
CBHW071120210326
41519CB00020B/6355